THE LITTLE

BOOK

Jewels for a Better Life

MELISSA LIEDKE

For my mother, who told me when I was going on my first job interview to say "yes" when asked if I could do anything, which led to my life motto –
"I can."

Table of Contents

Acknowledgements

I'd like to recognize the brilliant people who inspired me to find the best version of myself and then aspire to live it out in living color.

Beginning with Kyla Stinnett, writer extraordinaire, and the person I chose to edit my work. Kyla challenged me to use my words wisely but never tried to distract me from my voice, and she always corrected my grammar with aplomb.

A personal thanks and recognition to Erin Carenzo, an award-winning creative director, for designing my book cover. With 20+ years of experience crafting world-class content and promotions for television, film, and thought leaders, I count it a privilege to share her talent with my audience.

To Frank, Angella, Andrew, and Allen. The four reasons I keep reaching for the stars, and I am blessed and proud to call you "my family."

Throughout this book, you'll meet many people who stepped into my life for a moment in time, and encouraged, challenged, and mentored me. I'm eternally grateful!

Introduction

The renowned poet Maya Angelou once said, "Do the best you can until you know better. Then when you know better, do better." It starts with self-awareness and a willingness to set our ego aside for the greater good. Self-awareness can lead to changes that will help us become the best version of ourselves. And as Maya Angelou taught, we can do better when we know better. When we focus on *being* and commit to operating in a "best version" state, we naturally experience greater success in work and life.

My intention in writing this book is to share the "Be" Jewels (precious gems) that help me in my own life to know better so I could do better. The first gem I discovered is the secret to living an awesome life comes to each of us wrapped in a three-pound package called the brain; inside our brains are these awesome things called thoughts. Thoughts come to us in different forms such as music, ideas, and pictures. And guess what? We get to choose which thoughts we want to focus on – That means we can put our attention on the thoughts and ideas that we want to expand in our experience. It was a profound "gem" moment in time when I grasped the power of managing my thought patterns – it created a transformational chain of events that catapulted me to places I never dreamed of all because I chose to focus only on thoughts that served me best. Rhonda Byrne said, "Whatever you think about, you bring about." Think about that.

Be Brave

"You are braver than you believe."
-A.A. Milne

When I think about being brave, war heroes and first responders come to mind. I stand in awe of men and women who march to war knowing their lives are on the line. And the first responders who teeter over a bridge to save a mother and her child from a car ready to plunge into deep waters with one wrong move – that's bravery at its best.

I've never fought in a war or saved anyone's life, but I experienced fear and danger on a grand scale several years ago when the car I was riding in rounded a corner in downtown Bogota, Columbia, and the group I was with came face-to-face with two soldiers pointing machine guns at us. Although the machine guns were evidence enough, I knew we were really in danger when the passenger in the front seat, a missionary who had seen violence at the height of unrest in El Salvador, said, "Shit!" In case you didn't know, missionaries don't usually swear.

Paul, our driver and a missionary to Columbia, rolled down his window as one of the soldiers walked up to the car. Paul conversed with the soldier in Spanish while his buddy stood off to the side with his machine gun pointed in our direction. The rest of us sat there – quiet and still as though hoping to evade a rattlesnake waiting to snatch its prey. After what seemed like an eternity, we were allowed to leave.

As Paul drove away, there were audible sighs from everyone, along with a few expletives. Those of us who didn't speak Spanish asked Paul what had been said.

The soldier had asked Paul what we were doing in this part of town, and then told him, in no uncertain terms, that we had no business being there and that they could kill us – no questions asked. Militants had recently stormed the Colombian Palace and 120 people lost their lives, so there was no doubt in our minds that he meant what he said. We had entered a danger zone, and the gravity of our situation was not lost on any of us seated in the car that night.

Looking back on that moment, I didn't feel brave, but I'm grateful that Paul exhibited brave behavior in the way he interacted with the soldiers. He was respectful and calm, and he didn't waiver in his response to the soldier's questions. I could have succumbed to fear when the invitation to visit Columbia came my way. I was very aware of all the violence happening in that country, but I went anyway. I think that on some level, that was being brave (although some might say it was foolish). But I've always lived my life with the belief that I'm always in the right place at the right time doing the right thing. It was part of my life journey, and I learned that bravery is moving through fear for the sake of a higher goal. And I still feel grateful for our guardian angels protecting us from harm that night.

Although it may seem less threatening than being stopped at gunpoint, performing before an audience, whether it's one or one hundred, requires an act of bravery for most people. Did you know that Americans are more afraid of public speaking than they are of dying? That's serious fear. When I was ten years old I was afraid of dying, but I was more afraid of singing in church. One Sunday morning as I stood behind the pulpit getting ready to sing a duet with my aunt, I was overcome with fear. The only real danger in that moment was the humiliation I would have felt had I hyperventilated, fainted, and cracked my head open when I hit the floor. As the pianist played the introduction, I looked down at the music, my knees shook, and my head froze in the down position and stayed there – not once did I raise my eyes to the audience.

Somehow I made it through that performance and continued to sing, though I still remember that during the times I moved away from the pulpit and held the microphone to sing, my hands sweated so profusely that I believe I would have been electrocuted had it not been for the napkin folded tightly around the microphone to protect me from the flow of electricity pulsing through the metal device.

Despite my fearful behavior, my parents continued to encourage me in my mediocre talent, and I felt a new level of bravery each time I walked on to the platform to sing.

You might be asking, "If the fear is so great, why bother?" It's simple. When we commit to doing things outside our comfort zone, even if we fail, we have the potential to be exceptional human beings doing exceptional things. As one of the greatest basketball players of all time, Michael Jordan, once said,

"I've failed over and over and over again in my life, and that's why I succeed."

While I never became an Adele or a Barbara Streisand, I did learn three principles that helped me raise my head, make eye contact, and effectively use my talents in life and in the workplace:

1. Preparation Is King. Athletes memorize their playbook and do their daily drills. Piano students practice their scales every day. Language students learn grammar, memorize new vocabulary, and practice speaking with native speakers. Chefs who want to be the best study *The Professional Chef* guide from the Culinary Institute of America. When I wanted to improve my singing and performance skills, I worked with a voice coach to help me with stage fright, and I learned simple techniques that helped calm my nerves and project my voice in any setting. As an adult, I also joined Toastmasters to hone my public speaking skills.

The key to preparation is to find something or someone to inspire you. Get up close and personal, and emulate the thing they do best. I love to cook and decorate, and I took my homemaking skills to a whole new level when I got up close and personal with Martha Stewart, watching her every day on television. She inspired me on many levels even though I've never met her in person. She was what I affectionately call a "mentor unaware."

2. Practice with Intention. Baking is one of my favorite pastimes, and I love the original Nestlé Toll House® chocolate-chip cookie recipe. I could have read the recipe on the back of the package, opened the bag, smelled the semi-sweet chocolate chips, and imagined how great the cookies tasted, but until I actually made them, I didn't get to enjoy the experience and the final result.

To be great at anything, you must pull out the playbook of your choice and practice with the intention of being the very best. Like Michael Jordan, you'll probably fail over and over again, but he never gave up and neither should you. I've had many failures along the way. And some of my most notable ones have been in the kitchen. But I think my friends and family would tell you they remember more great meals than sorry ones. The disasters are now fun dinner conversations – like the times (yes, it happened more than once) I served shoe leather to guests for dinner because I hadn't figured out the whole low-slow-long technique for cooking cheap cuts of meat.

3. Performing Is Rewarding. This is what I call the "be brave" phase. You've prepared and practiced, and it's time get up and do it. Whether it's in a one-on-one setting with your manager or to a large audience, this is your opportunity to showcase your efforts and abilities with the intention of educating, inspiring, or motivating others. Also, the personal satisfaction and joy you feel from doing whatever makes your heart sing is enormously gratifying. And who doesn't love it when someone validates your talent with applause and a request to share your knowledge with others? For an athlete, it's the roar from stadium crowds, and for the performer, it's the encore. The encore can serve as a humble affirmation that you are on the right path and living the best version of yourself.

Like Michael Jordan, embrace your failures, and when you falter, do as Ella Hicks, the "Rebel Thriver," says, "If you stumble, make it part of the dance." Ice dancers do it all the time. And guess what? At some point you will stumble. We all do. But remember that the audience is cheering you on – they want you to succeed, so get right back up, go forth, and let yourself shine.

"You can fail at what you don't want so you might as well take a chance at doing what you love."

———

JIM CARREY

Be Smart

*"You are far too smart to be the
one thing standing in your way."*
-Jennifer J. Freeman

As a new analyst at American Airlines, the first time I presented a monthly update for my market to the Vice President of Yield Management was a milestone in my career. I know my colleagues, mostly Ivy Leagues graduates with MBAs, must have been surprised. But quite frankly, I was equally surprised at what I had accomplished in less than two years at the company. My assumption was that they had no expectations of me because I had no training of any kind, so when I did succeed, they were probably all scratching their heads, and thinking, "Wow, she did it. That's amazing!" In reality, I think they saw something in me that I didn't, and became my champions.

My journey to self-awareness began when I realized I was potentially standing in the way of my own success. I started out making $6.20 an hour in a department informally known as "Central Reject," which could have easily described my life by some people's standards. I dropped out of college to get married and hadn't aspired to anything beyond motherhood, cookbooks, and Southern Living Magazines up to that point. Don't get me wrong – I think motherhood is the noblest of professions, and I was very proud of my role. But when my children were in grade school, I had a friend with two boys in college, and I watched her mourn when they left home to live their lives as adults. She had poured her life into them and was traumatized when they left home and didn't look back. I decided, right then and there, that I needed a life outside of my children. So when the opportunity to work at American Airlines presented itself, I took it. It was a humble start to what turned out to be a fulfilling career.

Training for Central Reject meant spending six weeks learning a computer system called Sabre so that we could eventually correct rejected American Airlines itineraries booked by other airlines when they came into the system. There were three of us in the training class: me, Barb, and Carol, who just happened to have a photographic memory. When Barb and I realized what we were up against, we had minor panic attacks at the thought of testing alongside this person who could flip through flashcards with city codes just one time, and make a perfect, or near perfect, score when tested.

The challenge was on. We were not about to be shown up by a nineteen-year-old smarty-pants, albeit one of the nicest smarty-pants you could ever meet. We studied as if our lives depended on it and, when it was all said and done, the instructor told us we were the highest-performing class she'd ever taught. The significance of that statement was not lost on me because I knew I performed better because the bar had been set high and I'd accepted the challenge. Each time I tested, my goal was to beat my last score.

One of the first people I met when I started in Central Reject was Josephine, an opinionated German woman who didn't suffer fools gladly. She had impeccable style and a work ethic befitting the World War II era in which she grew up. Despite being only a few years from retirement, Josephine showed up for work on time every day and worked circles around her much younger colleagues. For some unknown reason, she liked me and took me under her wing.

Josephine recognized something in me that I had no idea existed, and I give her full credit for bringing out the smart in me. Remember, I had been a stay-at-home mom for years, and *Sesame Street* and Winnie-the-Pooh had been my life up to this point, so what ensued under Josephine's tutelage shocked and inspired me. After working alongside her for several months, she approached me one day and said, "You're too smart for this department. When your year is up, I want you to apply for a job in the Yield Management day-of-departure operations group."

Still in mommy mode, I was stunned that she thought I could get a job in that group. Yield Management was one of the most prestigious departments in the company, and I thought only college graduates were considered for any position there. Unbeknownst to me, and lucky for me and many other employees, American Airlines didn't consider a college degree a requirement for success. In that moment though, I thanked her for her confidence in me, and said the obligatory "okay," never thinking I'd actually do it. But true to form, when my one-year anniversary came around, Josephine showed up at my desk and reminded me to apply for the job. I applied and was invited to participate in a group interview, which meant three to five interviewers on one side of the table, and three to five interviewees on the other side of the table. Imagine my surprise when I got the job!

Back to those Ivy League colleagues I told you about earlier. When I transitioned into the Yield Management group, I had the privilege of working with a group of über-smart people who brought me up ten levels. They were brilliant, and like Josephine, my Ivy League colleagues took me under their wings and coached me to new levels. After three years and another promotion, it was time to move on. On my last day in the group, I gave my final presentation to the vice president, and when I was done she congratulated me on my promotion to my new job in FlyAAway Vacations. She told me, "Go do great things in tours and come back to Yield Management." Talk about a confidence builder!

Once I realized that my personal success depended on me recognizing my smarts and getting out of my own way, I was able to take my career to a new level by applying the following three principles:

1. Be Coachable. When you start a new job, ask your manager to challenge you to be the best that you can be, and then be a producer of excellent work. I learned early on in my career to let my managers know when I started a new job that I wanted to be challenged to be my very best. Managers love to hear that from their employees, and they will work hard to help you be successful.

One of my greatest lessons in this area happened early in my career. I had been in one of my favorite jobs at American Airlines for about a year when a new manager came on the scene. With her she brought an employee from her previous group who I quickly bonded with. She was smart, full of positive energy and we fast became friends and great work colleagues. She had been promoted under the new manager in her previous group so I was very interested to learn as much as I could about her experience because I was looking for that next promotion. My new colleague and friend coached and encouraged me along the way and by the time reviews came around, I was feeling as confident as one could feel about getting to the next level. The day came for my review, she gave me one last high-five and said "You've got this." and off I went. My review went very well up to the point where my manager had checked the box that said, "YOU'RE NOT GETTING PROMOTED." There were plenty of adjectives to describe the way I felt in that moment but let's go with "shock" and "devastated" for now. I fumbled my way through the rest of the session, left the conference room, grabbed my purse, drove home and threw myself across my bed and sobbed. I wailed and wondered allowed, "How could this have happened?" My friend who had been promoted under her coached me to perfection so what went wrong? You're right, I was talking to the wrong person. While my colleague was a great source of inspiration and encouragement, she wasn't in control of my career destiny – duh! After about twenty minutes of self-pity, I picked myself up off the bed, dried my tears, fixed my make up and went back to work. A few days later, I scheduled a meeting with my manager and did what I should have done in the first place, and that was to talk to her about my career goals and getting to the next level. After a very productive conversation about timing and readiness, within a few months I made it to the next level.

Sidebar

Tip: When you're at work, work. I remember walking by one of my colleague's desk every morning and seeing her reading her Bible instead of working. My perception was that she wanted to be seen as being "spiritual" when, in fact, she was stealing company time. Enough said about that.

2. Make Your Connections Count. Are the people you work with and for helping you on your road to personal achievement? If not, connect with new people who inspire and motivate you to tap into more of your infinite potential. I always told my children, "You become who you hang around." You don't have to look far to find idiots; they're lurking around every corner. You may have to go farther down the path to find the smart people, but go the extra mile – it's one the greatest gifts you can give yourself.
3. Pay It Forward. Be the Josephine in someone else's life. Look for, recognize, and acknowledge attributes of greatness in others. Jack Lemmon, an acclaimed and beloved actor nominated eight times for an Academy Award with two wins to his name, told other aspiring actors "If you're lucky enough to do well, it's your responsibility to send the elevator back down."

It doesn't matter where you are in your life or career, there's always someone in your sphere of influence that can benefit from your knowledge and encouragement. It can be something as simple as showing a new employee how to navigate the intra-company website, sharing your technical expertise, or encouraging a colleague to go for that promotion. As Martha Stewart would say, "It's a good thing."

Jack Lemmon was offered the role in Cool Hand Luke in 1967 and he turned it down because he felt the role was better suited for Paul Newman. The rest of the story is his production company produced the film so it would have been easy for him to keep it all to himself.

The key to being successful at paying it forward is to check your ego at the door, and do your part to shine the light on greatness. Anything you give will come back to you many times over.

"Be so good they can't ignore you."

―――――――――

STEVE MARTIN

Be Happy

"Many assume my business success has brought me happiness. But the way I see it, I am successful because I am happy."
-Richard Branson

I've never met Richard Branson, but I'm guessing that behind that big, contagious smile he carries with him everywhere he goes, there are some painful life stories. Yet they certainly haven't affected his happiness.

If you met my friend Emily, you couldn't help but feel her exceptional energy and joy because she is one of the happiest people I know. She has a successful career doing what she loves to do. She goes home every night to one of the nicest men on the planet who would give his right arm for her. Her two children are the light of her life and are living healthy, happy grown-up lives. Did I mention she has three dogs and a cat that adore her? They vie for her attention and curl up at her feet every evening as she finishes her day with a glass of wine in one of the four rocking chairs on her deck overlooking the six acres of awesomeness that she calls home.

You're probably thinking, *If I had all that I would be happy too.* But you see, that's only part of her story. Before Emily turned 40 she was diagnosed with breast cancer. Like so many women, she endured the trauma of chemotherapy and the effects of living without lymph nodes, and countless reconstructive surgeries. A few years into her recovery, her mother was crossing the street in a little town in Alabama while on vacation, and was hit by a sixteen-year-old boy driving too fast. She was at her dad's side when he had to make the painful decision to remove her from life support. During these difficult years, Emily took custody of her niece and nephew after her younger sister chose a life of addiction that left a gaping hole in the fabric of her children's lives. She knew her niece and nephew deserved a "mom and dad" so, against her father's wishes, she made the tough decision to place them with a loving family in an open adoption. Then a few years later, her dad, a non-smoker, succumbed to lung cancer.

The remarkable part about Emily's story is that throughout these traumatic events she has never once played the victim card or lost her joy. Her optimism about life is contagious and her glass is always half full. I believe that like Richard Branson, Emily is successful in life because she's happy.

I think happiness is a choice, and one of the best reasons to choose happiness is that we're nicer people when we're happy. I look for inspiration in people like Richard Branson and my friend Emily, and following are three tips that can help you expand your happiness at work and in life:

1. Keep Smiling. As Louis Armstrong sang, "When you're smiling, the whole world smiles with you." Smiling is contagious. Scientific studies have proven there are physical and emotional health benefits to smiling. Years ago, I worked for a dentist as an office manager, and his main rule was to greet each patient with a big smile. That smile was more important than the matching boutique outfits his wife selected at the beginning of each season for the office staff to wear. So before you leave the house each morning, look in the mirror and put on your best

accessory – a great big smile. I like to keep a mirror at my desk to not only check my lipstick throughout the day, but to check my smile too.

2. Be Positive. Think of the most negative person in your life. How do you feel when you're around this individual? I dislike being around negative people because it's too easy to mirror their behavior and become the thing I hate the most. Negative people abound in every workplace, and while we can't escape them, we can minimize the effect they have on our world. If you're positive, and choose only to say good things about your company and the people who work there, the curmudgeons will run because they need negative energy to feed their negativity.

3. Assume the Best. Plato once said, "Be kind, for everyone you meet is fighting a hard battle." His words remind me of the community manager I had to work with when I served on the board for my Home Owners Association. My first impression of her was questionable – she seemed hard and defensive. I assumed it was because she had to deal with demanding homeowners who didn't read the bylaws and constantly broke the rules. But as I got to know her, I learned that she'd recently experienced the tragic loss of a sibling and of her best friend who she had known since grade school. Not only did she have to deal with annoying homeowners but, in the midst of it all, she was grieving. My whole perspective changed and I began to see her in a totally different light. Remember, you never know what's going on in someone's life so assume the best until they prove otherwise.

"Great minds discuss ideas;
average minds discuss events;
small minds discuss people."

———

ELEANOR ROOSEVELT

Be Present

*"You create a good future
by creating a good present."
-Eckhart Tolle*

Lilly is three years old, and this is how one exceptional Monday started out:

Lilly: "Mamma, this tables gotta turn pink tomorrow with sparkles like your favorite color."

Mom: "Oh yeah? Really?"

Lilly: "Yeah, it's gonna turn pink for you."

Mom: "Okay."

Lilly: "Orange is my favorite color."

Mom: "That's a nice color. Ally (Lilly's two-year-old sister), what's your favorite color?"

Lilly: "Her favorite color is purple."

Mom: "Purple?"

Lilly: "Yes, purple is her favorite color."

Despite the fact that Lilly is living with her mom and sister in a women's shelter, far away from the troubled life her mom chose to rescue herself and two daughters from, she doesn't wake up each morning and ponder the bad stuff from yesterday. In the bedroom on the second floor inside the shelter, her world is filled with possibilities that include magical moments filled with lots of color – and chocolate. And she fully expects that table to turn pink and sparkle at the appointed time.

Lilly, not yet tainted by the effects of adulthood, doesn't have a mind corrupted by negative thought patterns – she lives her life in the present. Therefore, she can't be depressed or anxious because it hasn't occurred to her yet to dwell on the past or stress about what's going to happen tomorrow – both prescriptions for making things worse than they actually are. Beyond momentary tiffs with her sister and negotiating naptime and chocolate breaks with her mom and Gigi (a.k.a Grandma), Lilly wakes up every day with an unconscious expectation that everything will go well in her world.

Lilly's story is a poignant reminder for all of us who have moved from the innocence of childhood, where we lived in a magical, pure-minded state, into adulthood, where havoc with our mind ensues daily. We walk backwards, battling yesterday's woes, lecturing and arguing with perceived enemies both past and present, and imagining in great detail and in living color all the things that could go wrong tomorrow.

"If you are depressed, you are living in the past. If you are anxious, you are living in the future. if you are at peace, you are living in the present."
-Lao Tzu

Several years ago I worked for a married couple who were both therapists, and I watched them put an unhappy period in their marriage on display every time they stepped on the platform to teach other couples a better way to communicate. It was a method of communication that saved their marriage, and they wanted to share it with others. During each session, they walked back in time and shared the woes they suffered being married to each other during those

21

difficult years – the tension on stage was high as they relived those moments over and over and over again. And when the lights on stage went out, despite the techniques they used to save their marriage all those many years ago, it was apparent things weren't so rosy on the home front. As I observed their behavior on and off stage over a period of several months, I realized the irony in their attempt to help others: they were hurting themselves by reliving the past experiences that almost cost them their marriage in the beginning. I thought to myself, *They need to get a divorce. But wait, they can't, because it would go against everything they were teaching.* So in essence, it seemed they were stuck with no reasonable way out. Their behavior on stage was a major "aha" moment for me – constantly dragging the past into your present can be a detriment to your present and future.

Knowing that during your lifetime, you will interact with your work family as much or more than your personal family, how is it possible to take life one day at a time and live in such a way that a "good present" is your norm – at work and in life? Here are some practices that have helped me and many other people do just that.

1. Quiet Your Mind. The best way to set yourself up for success every day and live in a peaceful, joyous state is to manage your mind through meditation. The practice of meditation can help you cultivate a sense of inner calm even when you encounter difficult people and situations.

I once worked with a lady in an organization who was brilliant at her job, but she was never able to get to the level she wanted because of the way she treated her fellow employees. Her job required her to address questions and interact with people regularly, but her colleagues approached her with fear and trepidation, dreading the retribution and outburst of anger she would spew at them if they caught her off guard. Even though she could be extremely nice and genial at times, it never made up for the havoc she created in her "off moments" – in fact, it only complicated matters because people never knew from interaction to interaction who they would be dealing with – Dr. Jekyll or Ms. Hyde.

I would have fared much better in my interactions with this woman had I been setting aside time each morning to prepare myself mentally through meditation. I know because since that time, I've encountered people like her in other organizations. But now that mindfulness principles are a non-negotiable part of my daily living, I am able to separate myself from other people's drama and interact with them while remaining calm and centered.

If you've ever worked with a difficult person whose negative energy takes up all the space in a room, you have probably fantasized about living in a log cabin in the woods, far away from society – or perhaps on a private island in a remote part of the world. In reality, you can't avoid all difficult people all the time, nor can you control the way they act. The only person you can control is *you*. However, you can prepare yourself to deal with difficult people and situations, and remain so calm that interacting with them will not hurt your ability to perform well in your job and enjoy your life.

I want to offer a caveat by saying that there are people with personality disorders who wreak havoc on organizations every day. If you've ever had to deal with them, you know exactly what I'm talking about. Here are a few notable characteristics of people in this category: they react with emotional volatility, pit employees against each other, dominate the conversation, speak ill of everyone, act friendly one day and hostile the next day, blame others when things go wrong, and think nothing of letting an innocent person take the fall. Finally, they lead with a high sense of entitlement and disregard rules and social norms. Even if you have excellent interpersonal skills, they can make you question your own sanity and leave you thinking that everything is your fault.

If you find yourself working for or with a person in this category, don't think you can win or be the hero for your organization – leave that to the professionals. In my experience, human resource departments are slow or non-responsive when it comes to dealing with these kinds of difficult people for several reasons. Sometimes employees are understandably afraid to complain. In other cases, despite their extreme dysfunction, difficult people provide a valuable service (they tend to be very intelligent) so their abnormal behavior is overlooked. And, finally, they could be closely connected to and protected by someone above your pay grade. So, if you find yourself in an intolerable situation, my best advice is to keep your head down and produce the best work possible while you search for another job.

The good news is that you can learn to cultivate calm and stay centered, even in the midst of chaos, through the practice of meditation. As an enormous and growing body of scientific research shows, meditation is a powerful way to improve your emotional well-being and physical health. For example, a Harvard [1]research team, in conjunction with Massachusetts General Hospital, led 16 participants in an 8-week Mindfulness-based Stress Reduction (MBSR) Program. MRI's of each participant's brain were taken (including the control group), two weeks before the program launched and at the completion of the study.

The meditation group spent, on average, 27 minutes a day practicing mindfulness exercises, and in the post-survey all the meditating participants reported significant improvements compared with the control group. The most fascinating aspect of this study was the finding that the meditation group showed an increase in grey matter density in the hippocampus. This area of the brain is recognized as an important factor for learning and memory, and is also associated with self-awareness, compassion, and personal reflection. In addition, the meditation group noted reductions in stress, and this correlated with decreased grey matter in the amygdala, known to play an important role in anxiety and stress.

The idea that we can transform the structure of our brain matter, and in turn improve our physical, mental, and emotional well-being, is quite remarkable. And in our hectic, multitasking, technology-driven world, it is more important than ever to find the time to meditate to expand our personal well-being and ability to deal with difficult people and situations.

Think of meditation as strength training for your brain. Like any form of exercise, you don't have to, nor should you, attempt to start out like an expert. You

---

[1] https://news.harvard.edu/gazette/story/2011/01/eight-weeks-to-a-better-brain/

don't need to join a monastery or sit in silence for hours on end to receive the benefits of meditation, including stress relief and feelings of bliss.

If meditation is not currently part of your daily routine, here is a simple meditation practice focusing on your breath that you can try right now.

Breathing Meditation

It goes without saying that oxygen is the most critical element of life. Because breathing is a natural bodily function, it's easy to take it for granted and develop the habit of breathing shallowly, which deprives us of oxygen and increases our stress response. It's important to foster healthy breathing habits, and we accomplish this by moving from shallow breathing to deep, belly breathing.

- Sit in a comfortable position and breathe in slowly to the count of 4. Now hold your breath for 6 seconds, and then release it to the count of 8. Do this a few times, focusing on each inhalation, each pause, and each exhalation.
- By focusing on each breath, you are training your mind to stay in the present. It is normal for random thoughts to show up during a meditative practice. When this occurs, don't fight against it – allow the thoughts to flow through and simply redirect your focus back on your breath.

Smell Your Flower and Blow Out Your Candle

When my daughter's children were very little and on the verge of a meltdown, she could help them return to a state of calm in just a few moments with a simple breathing exercise. She would tell them that they had an imaginary flower in one hand and an imaginary candle in the other. She kneeled to their level, looked them in the eye, and had them hold their imaginary flower under their noses. She would say, "Smell your flower." Then she would tell the children to turn to their other hand and say, "Now, blow out your candle."

Instead of saying, "Stop crying!" she engaged them in an activity designed to draw their focus away from the drama and breathe, deeply inhaling and exhaling. Sometimes they had to blubber their way through the exercise several times before the drama subsided, but it worked every time. And, in fact, it had a positive effect on mom because she was doing the breathing exercise right along with them, and it helped her to remain calm while she was calming them.

Creating a Daily Meditation Practice

When you're establishing a daily meditation practice, it helps to make it a routine and pay attention to two important elements: time and space.

- Time. Set aside 15 minutes each morning when the world is quiet and your mind is in its most restful, clear state. If you meditate soon after waking, it will quickly become a non-negotiable part of your day, helping you to begin your daily activities in a state of centered, restful awareness. Once you realize the benefits, you will not allow anything or anyone to interrupt you.

Consider your meditation a "gift of time" that you bestow on yourself each morning. Untie the ribbon, remove the wrapping paper, and relish each minute as if your quality of life depends on it – because it does.

- Space. Your meditation space can be a favorite chair in a quiet place in your home or, weather permitting, outdoors in a favorite setting that's peaceful and serene.

If you don't live alone, you may want to create a meditation space in an area where you can be alone for a few minutes. Get creative! Some people have converted closets, pantries, and other small spaces into a meditation sanctuary. Explain to your family ahead of time what you are doing and why. And when they see the sign on the door that says, "Meditating," they will learn to turn around and tiptoe out of the room.

I have a friend who takes a meditation walk every morning. Recently, he noted that he felt like his walks weren't working for him anymore and he realized that his new dog was a distraction. So, unless the people and pets in your life meditate with you, find a time when you can be completely alone.

If you feel like you need help, there are thousands of guided meditations online that you can use to create your own daily practice. Explore and find what resonates with you. And remember, when all else fails and you have one of those moments – smell your flower and blow out that candle.

2. Make Your Bed. U.S. Navy Adm. William H. McRaven[2], commander of the forces that led the raid to kill Osama bin Laden, said this during a

[2] https://www.ricklindquist.com/speeches/make-your-bed#:~:text=If%20you%20make%20your%20bed,turned%20into%20many%20tasks%20completed

commencement speech at the University of Texas:

"If you make your bed every morning, you will have accomplished the first task of the day. It will give you a small sense of pride, and it will encourage you to do another task, and another, and another. And by the end of the day, that one task completed will have turned into many tasks completed."

He went on to say, "The little things in life matter, and if you can't do the little things right in life, then you'll never be able to do the big things right."

I've noticed throughout my working career that, ever so often, I find myself in a "work fog," otherwise known as unproductive nothingness. I didn't connect the dots right away, but I began to notice a pattern that occurs when this happens. I pull out the Clorox wipes from my bottom desk drawer, clear my desk, and everything gets a good scrubbing; desktop, keyboard, phone – if it's on my desk, it gets sterilized. I finish up by cleaning out my inbox and purging old files.

"For every minute spent organizing, an hour is earned."
-Benjamin Franklin

Your personal space is a reflection of how you see yourself, and keeping your personal space in good order is an important part of looking after yourself and keeping your mind open and clear to right answers and inspiration. And it starts each morning when you make your bed.

3. Live in the Moment.[3] President Abraham Lincoln led the country in the deadliest war in U.S. history, in which almost half a million soldiers were killed. Compound that with grieving the loss of a beloved son and nurturing a wife battling mental illness, President Lincoln faced what, to some, would seem like insurmountable pain, loss, and stressor points. To make matters worse, he battled depression and lived in a constant state of melancholy throughout his life. Yet in spite of his profound inner and outer pain, he managed to find the strength to keep going. And, fortunately, he discovered the power of being present and embracing each day as it came. He found ways to compensate for his melancholy, including telling jokes and stories.

Mrs. Lincoln's dressmaker shared a story about President Lincoln coming in to the room where she was fitting Mrs. Lincoln one day. The President was openly sad and despondent. He lied down on a chaise, picked up his Bible, and read for awhile. After a bit, he put his open Bible down and left the room. Curious, she glanced over to see what he had been reading and saw that it was open to the book of Job. Job was a man who went from riches to rags, practically overnight. He lost everything: children, property, wealth, his health, and even his good name. Things were so bad that his wife told him he should just bless God and die. But Job didn't die and he never gave up hope. I would like to think that President Lincoln read Chapter 42 that day and found hope in

_____

[3] https://www.americamagazine.org/faith/2020/10/27/abraham-lincoln-book-of-job-civil-war-bible-united-states

the ending; Job's life as he knew it was completely restored and then some. He lived another 144 years and "died, being old and full of his days."

"The best thing about the future is that it comes only one day at a time."
-Abraham Lincoln

In the face of immense hardship on all fronts, President Lincoln's accomplishments were prodigious, and he is still recognized by scholars and the American people as one of the greatest Presidents in U.S. history.

Like President Lincoln and many others who have struggled with difficult situations, we have the ability to decide how we will focus our attention and move forward.

If you find yourself in a state of emotional upset or unsteadiness, take a minute to think about what you are thinking about. Take stock of what you're choosing to dwell on and then focus on clearing your thoughts and engaging in activities that can help keep you in the present:

- Watch funny movies.
- Volunteer at your favorite charity.
- Do random acts of kindness.
- Write down three things you are thankful for every day.
- Take a nap.

One of my favorite artists, Jason Mraz, penned a song titled "Living in the Moment." The song talks about "laying traps that we put in our path." Notice that he says "we." He doesn't say that other people are laying traps in our way – we do it to ourselves. He goes on to say . . .

"I will not waste my days making up all kinds of ways to worry about all the things that will not happen to me. I'm letting myself off the hook for things I've done. I let my past go past and now I'm having fun. And if I fall asleep, I know you'll be the one who'll always remind me to live in the moment."

So, here I am reminding you to stay present and do more than just live in the moment – stay present and make every moment count.

"It is a mistake to look too far ahead.
The chain of destiny can only be grasped one link at
a time."

───────────

SIR WINSTON CHURCHILL

Be Curious

*"I have no special talent.
I am only passionately curious."*
-Albert Einstein

Albert Einstein is recognized as the most influential physicist of the 20th century. What if Albert Einstein's mother had listened to the teacher who relegated him to the "addled" group, and forced him to remain in a classroom driven by harsh rules, complete with corporal punishment for minor infractions? Thankfully, she took him home and provided a learning environment that fostered his curious, highly intelligent mind. From that starting point, he did the work and transformed our understanding of the laws of nature and the way light, gravity, and time behave.

Throughout history, innovations that changed the world in dramatic ways were inspired by curious minds. Someone said, "I wonder?" and curiosity led to many accidental discoveries that changed the course of human history – like the transistor and penicillin.

In 1250, Roger Bacon's curiosity about mirrors and the principles of reflection and refraction led to the invention of the magnifying glass. Magnifying lenses not only helped people see clearly, but also became the impetus for breakthroughs in the fields of astronomy, biology, archeology, optometry, and surgery.

In 1440, Johannes Gutenberg inspired the Age of Enlightenment by making books available and affordable to lower socio-economic groups with a machine that could print up to 3,600 pages per day.

By 1600, Gutenberg presses had printed more than 200 million new books. People now had access to the written word, and as the cost of books dropped, literacy levels rose. As new ideas took hold, for better or worse, people began to challenge authority as never before. This surge of independent thinking eventually undermined the authority of the church and the monarchy, paving the way for political revolutions in the 18th and 19th centuries.

"What the world is today, good and bad, it owes to Gutenberg."
-Mark Twain

In 1698, Thomas Savery invented the steam-powered water pump. This basic application of energy-into-motion fueled one of the most significant leaps in technology the world has ever seen, paving the way for combustion engines and jet turbines. This single invention gave rise to cars and aircraft in the 20th century.

The 18th and 19th centuries delivered a whirlwind of advancement, and innovations during this time period catapulted society to previously unimaginable places. For example, Alessandra Volta is credited with creating the first electrical battery. In the early 1800s, he proved that electricity could be generated with chemicals. Up until that point, it had been theorized that electricity was only generated by living beings.

In 1831, Michael Faraday used electricity to build the first power generator. That led to the first long-lasting incandescent light bulb, invented in 1878 by Joseph Swan and Thomas Edison. Think about how electricity impacts your life today and what it's like when there's a power outage. Life as we know it stalls.

In 1856, Sir Henry Bessemer, an inventor and engineer, developed a method for manufacturing steel inexpensively. The "Bessemer process" kicked off the Industrial Revolution in America and helped the United States become one of the world's biggest economies. Steel gave us bridges, railroads, skyscrapers, and engines.

One of my favorite rides at Disneyworld is the Carousel of Progress. It takes you on a journey through time and showcases the innovations that took place during my grandmother's lifetime. She lived to the age of 92, and her generation experienced innovation and "firsts" in a way that no generation before or after has seen. Electricity extended daylight and delivered automation in the home with time-saving appliances, indoor plumbing ended the inconveniences of outhouses, automobiles replaced horse and buggies, and travel to distant places became the norm with buses, trains, and planes. And who would have ever thought you could pick up the handle on a little black device called a "telephone" and talk to someone many miles away? The radio broadcast the spoken word into homes and was soon joined by another box-shaped device with four legs called the "television." Viewers could actually see people interacting with each other. Mind-boggling.

And let's not forget space travel. In my grandmother's lifetime she went from using candles and kerosene lamps to light her world when the sun went down to watching Neil Armstrong and Buzz Aldrin climb out of a space capsule and take a walk on the moon.

None of these amazing things would have happened if someone had not been curious.

Curiosity also plays an important role in brain stimulus, and scientific studies have shown the far-reaching health benefits of nurturing your mind.

"If one can remain intellectually active and stimulated throughoutone's lifespan, that's protective against late-life dementia. Staying mentally active is definitely good for your brain."
-David Knopman, professor of neurology
at the Mayo Clinic

The important takeaway from this look back at history is that smart people with curious minds did the work that propelled the world to new heights. It's more than just sitting in wonderment. It starts with a question that leads to inspired action. Here are a few ways to spark your own curiosity and sense of wonder.

1. Observe and Take Notes. Sir Alexander Fleming, a Scottish biologist, was curious about antibacterial substances. In 1928, while working on the influenza virus, he observed that mold had settled on a staphylococcus culture and formed a bacteria-free circle around itself. Rather than throwing it out thinking it was ruined, he took the time to observe and note what was actually happening and discovered that the mold had prevented the bacteria from growing. Because of his keen observation and good note taking, we now have penicillin.

My cousin is head of the biology department at a well-known college in the Midwest, and she relishes the times when she gets to take her students to remote areas around the world for weeks, learning through the power of observation and excellent note taking what can be achieved when curiosity takes over.

Remember Lilly's sister, Ally, whose favorite color is purple because Lilly said so? Ally may let Lilly dictate her favorite color right now because, at two years old, she's too busy observing everything around her. Ally's favorite word is "Wow!" followed by "Look at that!"

So, be an Ally, and wow yourself. Get passionate about something, take notes, catalog your findings, and let curiosity abound in your world. Never stop wondering.

2. Try Lots of Different Things. For anyone who thinks there's only one path to success, let me introduce you to my hero, Benjamin Franklin. He was a writer, inventor, scientist, diplomat, and successful businessman. And lest we forget, as one of the founding fathers of the United States of America, he helped write the Declaration of Independence and the United States Constitution. He even landed a premier position on U.S. currency, where his picture graces the $100 bill.

If upbringing is a predictor of success, Benjamin Franklin should have been a colossal failure. He was the youngest of 15 children, and his formal education ended when he was just ten years old, when he went to work in his father's candle-making business. His father soon recognized his son's boredom, and fearful he would head out to sea like his other siblings had done, sent him to work as an apprentice at the printing company owned by one of his older sons. Franklin's brother was abusive and beat him on a regular basis, doing everything in his power to block his brother's success as a writer and refusing to publish any of his work.

None of these challenges, however, stopped Franklin from becoming the absolute best version of himself. On the contrary, the hardships in his life seemed to be his propellant for greatness. Obstacles were his "friend," and he regularly accepted the challenge to find solutions that led him down many different career paths during his lifetime.

Once Franklin escaped his brother's abuse, he continued to work in publishing and became famous for his humor and wit in the political essays and other pamphlets he wrote on a regular basis. He eventually bought *The Pennsylvania Gazette* and published *Poor Richard's Almanac.*

Franklin is also recognized as one of the most prolific inventors of his time, and his remarkable contributions to society extend across many different avenues in the fields of medicine, science, philosophy, business, and government. You may remember him for his experiments with a kite and electricity, which led to his invention of the lightening rod. But did you know he also invented the wood-burning stove, bifocal glasses, a flexible catheter, and a musical instrument known as Franklin's Armonica? This eclectic group of inventions and many more were born out of need, whether his own or that of someone in his personal circle. An ardent sense of observation and curiosity abounded in every aspect of his life, and he continued to invent new things even after he retired from public life. Two notable inventions served him well in his personal library filled with a vast collection of books: a chair that flipped to become a step stool, and a pole that he could use to grasp books high above his head.

Franklin was a popular dude wherever he went, and as U.S. Ambassador to France, he was more than just a representative of the United States – he was a beloved figure. When he passed away, France mourned Franklin with all the pomp and ceremony normally given to a hero of their country.

So, if you're easily bored, don't listen to the naysayers who believe success means you have to work really, really hard at one thing for your entire life. Be the next Benjamin Franklin, try lots of different things, and have fun doing it. If you love what you're doing, it won't feel like work even if it's hard.

3. Believe in the Impossible. I can't tell you how many times I've heard people – a.k.a. "Negative Nellie" and "Pragmatic Polly" – say, "Oh, that's impossible because . . ." and give ten reasons to validate their flawed thinking.

"Why, sometimes I've believed as many as six impossible things before breakfast."
-Alice from Alice in Wonderland

Back in the 1990s when people were told they had to retire at 65, I read a story in the newspaper about a lawyer who at 50 years old decided he wanted to become a physician. So he quit his law practice, enrolled in medical school, and started practicing medicine at the age of 60. I bet he was one of those guys who, like Alice, got up every morning and believed six impossible things before he had his first cup of tea.

40

During my research, I came upon the story of another guy just like the lawyer-turned-doctor, Dr. Nicodemus, whose definition of retirement is "Doing what you want to do, and this is what I want to do." Dr. Nicodemus had a very successful career as a biomechanical engineer. He was director of spine research at the University of Texas Medical Branch, where he worked alongside orthopedic surgeons to understand the mechanics of the spine and develop instruments to repair damaged vertebrae. That led him to become interested in non-surgical treatments to treat back pain, which led him right through the front door of Michigan State University College of Osteopathic medicine where, at the age of 61, he was the oldest medical student graduate in history.

Get inspired and be an "Alice in Wonderland" – get up every morning and dream up six impossible things before you eat breakfast.

"Remember to look up at the stars and not down at your feet. Try to make sense of what you see and wonder what make the universe exist. Be curious. There is always something you can do and succeed at."

STEPHEN HAWKING

Be Focused

*"Rather than always focusing on what's urgent,
learn to focus on what is really important."*
-Stephen Covey

On April 17, 2016, [4]Kyle Schwarber's worst nightmare happened. Two games into the season with the Chicago Cubs, his outfield collision with teammate Dexter Fowler left him with a shredded knee that, by all accounts, meant he would be out of the game for the rest of the season.

As a young player who had proven himself worthy to play with the big boys, Kyle understood the severity of his situation as he left the field that day, but as history would bear witness, Kyle Schwarber would become known in baseball circles as the "comeback kid." And it all came down to one thing: deliberate focus.

It was Kyle's ability to hit the ball that got him in to the major leagues. In his last two years with the Indiana Hoosiers, he batted .362 with 32 homers in 120 games. In baseball terms that is better than good. But having been compared to a 1920s-era refrigerator because of his square physique, there were concerns that he couldn't do anything else. He wasn't a base stealer and his defense left much to be desired, but he could hit the ball so well that Club president, Theo Epstein, believed he was worthy and welcomed him into the Cubs' family with open arms.

After his on-field calamity, Mr. Epstein knew Kyle's game-playing days weren't over and, when trade

---

[4] https://www.cbsnews.com/news/how-chicago-cubs-finally-won-the-world-series-after-108-years/

rumors started swirling around, he made sure to let Kyle know he was enough and wasn't going anywhere. Mr. Epstein told him:

"There's no way we will trade you, all right? "You got hurt as a Cub. You're rehabbing as a Cub. You're going to come back and drop a homer on someone on Opening Day next year as a Cub.

You're a huge part of this team. You're coming back. Just wanted to tell you that."

With Mr. Epstein's pronouncement of support and a great team of doctors, Kyle continued in his recovery. As Mr. Epstein told Kyle, he fully expected him to be back on opening day the next year. So imagine his and everyone else's surprise when Kyle was cleared by his doctors to hit again during the current season. In less than six months, he managed to end up on the roster as a designated hitter for the 2016 World Series.

He was back and ready to play ball, but the big question was, could he actually hit the ball? A significant part of being a great hitter is the ability to identify one of the seven different types of pitches coming from the pitcher's mound – whether it's a fastball, curve ball, cutter, changer, slider, sinker, or a screwball. Kyle had been out of practice for almost six months, and while his knee was in good shape, how was his ability to see and recognize the kind of balls being thrown his way? To make matters worse, his doctors had limited him to 60 swings a day, meaning he couldn't physically practice by hitting balls. He had to save those swings for the actual games.

Kyle had a plan though, and it all came down to retraining his eyes through deliberate focus. He had the batting machine set up to pitch the different balls normally thrown at him, and for two hours a day leading up to that moment when he stepped up to bat for the first time after being injured, he observed pitches go by – over and over and over again. He didn't hit the balls. He just observed them with the intention of retraining his eyes to identify what was coming his way. No one had ever done this before, so it wasn't clear if observing balls for two hours at a time would be a good substitute for actually hitting balls. To encourage himself in this comeback endeavor, he told himself, *You know, I'm a good hitter, like I can do this.*

It worked. Kyle became the first Major League position player to get his first hit of the season during the World Series. Not only that, his team went on to defeat the Indians and claim the Cubs' first World Series championship in 108 years. It wasn't an easy win – the teams were tied six to six after nine innings and a rain delay stopped the game, but in the end, the Cubs took home the trophy. And Cubs manager, Joe Maddon, told reporters, "Without Kyle Schwarber, the Cubs would not have won the World Series."

Rather than focusing on what he did really well, what if Kyle had focused on being a better defensive player or stealing more bases? My guess is that he would have surely failed. Fortunately for the Cubs, he didn't. He was hyper focused on being the best in the one area in which he exceled – hitting balls.

Whether you're playing baseball, working your way up the corporate ladder, or starting your own company, like Kyle Schwarber, figure out what you're really good at and be deliberate in your approach to success:

1. Be a Uni-tasker. Technology has enabled us to take multitasking to a whole new level, but studies now show that trying to focus on more than one thing at a time is detrimental. For example, a study by the Institute of Psychiatry found that excessive use of technology reduces intelligence. The study found that participants who were distracted by incoming phone calls and emails experienced a dramatic 10-point drop in IQ – more than twice the effects of smoking marijuana, or the equivalent of losing one full night's sleep.

As a recovering multitasker, I used to take great pride in being able to accomplish more in a day than the average person because of my "awesome" ability to multitask at a very high level – I was a big-time bragger. Adding a smart phone to the mix only served to intensify my dysfunctional, multitasking behavior. Little did I know, I was dumbing myself down – literally.

How many times have you hit the send button on an email and forgotten the attachment because, well, you were engaged with a webinar or on a conference call and trying to do two things at once?

"If everything is important, then nothing is."
-Patrick Lencioni

Trying to do more than one thing at a time compromises the outcome of both and will likely produce mediocre results. There's also a high likelihood it will end up taking more time because of the do-over work required.

So, like Kyle Schwarber, put your blinders on and be deliberate by directing your focus towards the most important thing at that moment in time. And do it really well.

2. Anticipate Your Next Move. All you have to do to understand the importance of anticipating your next move is to get behind someone in the security check line at the airport who waits until they get up to the conveyor belt to begin the prep work required to go through security. Before arriving at this point, it's apparent they didn't pay one bit of attention to the security guard going up and down the line instructing people to discard water bottles; remove keys, wallets, change, and cellphones from their pockets; and place them along with laptops, shoes, and a Ziploc bag of acceptable liquids in the grey bins provided at the beginning of the line. Oh, and did I mention all the signs along the path with graphics displaying what was being communicated out loud by the security guard? There they stand, oblivious to the people behind them who listened and did the prep work, fumbling through their carry-on bags, pulling off their shoes, looking for a little white bowl to hold the contents of their pockets, and going backwards to find a grey tub. It's one of those "just shoot me now" moments because their decision to *not* pay attention and anticipate their next move doesn't just affect them, it slows down the process and affects everyone around them. Need I say more?

"The key is not to prioritize what's on your schedule, but to schedule your priorities."
-Stephen Covey

Once passengers are on the plane, flight attendants are quick to point out that their priority is safety for everyone sitting in those narrow, straight-back seats. Before the plane takes off, they take passengers through safety drills, and if you're seated in an exit row, they require you to look them in the eye and respond "yes" to their question about being able and willing to open the door if necessary. They don't wait until an event happens to prepare passengers for the worst-case scenario. They anticipate the worst-case scenario, prepare for it ahead of time, and when that's done, they serve refreshments.

So, anticipate your next move by having a plan and working the plan. Doing so will keep you in good stead with yourself and your colleagues, and you will find you have more time to enjoy the refreshments life has to offer.

3. Keep Moving Forward. Walt Disney experienced many roadblocks on his way to winning 22 Academy Awards and opening the most famous theme parks in the world: Disneyland in California and Disney World in Florida.

His first company went bankrupt so he and his brother moved to California and started over. A few years later, the distributor for one of his characters not only stole the rights to "Oswald the Lucky Rabbit" but also hired away the animators too. He and his brother regrouped again and went on to build a successful company with characters we're all familiar with, including Mickey Mouse, Minnie Mouse, Pluto, Goofy, the Three Little Pigs, and Snow White and the Seven Dwarfs.

In 1937, his efforts paid off, and Disney's first full-length animated movie, *Snow White and the Seven Dwarfs*, produced a whopping 1.4 billion dollars and took home eight Oscars – during the Great Depression! But after opening a new campus is 1937, Disney animators went on strike and many of them resigned. It took years to recover from this event.

> *"We keep moving forward, opening new doors, and doing new things, because we're curious and curiosity keeps leading us down new paths."*
> *-Walt Disney*

Walt Disney didn't let obstacles keep him from moving forward. With each setback, he lost someone or something in the fallout, but it didn't deter him. He forged ahead, and he had the ability to stay focused and move forward, accepting setbacks as a catalyst for new and bigger ideas.

Setbacks are an excellent way to get clarity and can help define next steps as you move forward in your life and career. They can also help you figure out what you want, so embrace them, and be grateful for the things you will learn about yourself and others.

If you find yourself encountering the same negative situations over and over again, then it's time to stop and get clarity. Write down the negative things that weigh you down on a daily basis. This will help you get clear on what you don't want. Because once you figure out what you don't want, you're on your way to knowing what you do want. Did you get that? Let me say it again – figuring out what you *don't* want will help you figure out what you *do* want.

Runners who jump hurdles on their way to the finish line know exactly what they want. They want to jump each hurdle they encounter with ease and be the first one to the finish line. It's that simple.

It took me about one week at one sales job to figure out that I hate selling. I am a results-oriented person and I hate talking on the phone. In this role, it could take six months to a year or more to close a deal, and it required lots of phone calls and long, quiet periods in between. I had never thought too much about what I liked to do because, up to that point, I had been in roles that catered to my strengths and things I enjoyed doing. This experience helped me realize that I really like projects that have a clear start and end.

Get crystal clear on what you want, do one thing at a time really well, and keep moving forward. And when obstacles show up in your path, you'll recognize them for what they are and be better able to clear a new path or maneuver around them with ease.

"You were born to win, but to be a winner,
you must plan to win, prepare to win, and expect
win."

ZIG ZIGLAR

Be Enough

You are enough. Let me repeat that so it goes through, You. Are. Enough.
-Marissa Peer

My first "real" job out of high school was at the Central National Life Insurance Company in Jacksonville, Illinois. On my first day, I showed up for work on time, nervous and STRESSED OUT. My responsibilities were basic administrative assistant duties, but you would have thought my assignment had me sitting with my finger on the nuclear button. At lunch I walked two blocks to town, headed straight to the lunch counter at Woolworths, and being too nervous to eat, ordered a large Coke. As I sat there sipping on my drink, I remembered a television commercial promoting Quiet World, an over-the-counter nerve pill of the day. *Hmm, that's just what I need,* thought the naive 17-year-old girl who didn't drink, smoke, or do drugs of any kind – legal or illegal. I headed down the "nerve pill" aisle, picked up a bottle of pills that promised to quiet my world, paid for them, and headed back to the office. I read the instructions and helped myself to two pills – on an empty stomach with a large Coke. What ensued next was a Seinfeld moment. My world got real quiet, and for the next four hours, I battled to keep my eyes open and stay upright in my chair. Sheer will and determination was the only thing that kept me from collapsing on the floor in a drug-induced stupor and having to be carted off to the hospital to have my stomach pumped.

What I really needed was for someone, anyone, to cup their hands on either side of my face, tell me to look them in the eye, and listen as they said, "Everything is okay and you are enough." And I needed to believe them.

The first time I watched Marissa Peer's Ted Talk on the topic of "being enough," I was fascinated by the simplicity of her message. Marissa is psychologist noted for her unique approach and ability to help the castoffs from her colleagues. When they have clients who don't respond to traditional methods, they send them to Marissa as a kind of last-ditch effort. Apparently, it's not uncommon to see limousines pull up in front of her residence carrying very successful people you and I would probably recognize. They come to her as broken souls and haters of self with one foot dangling off the cliff of life.

After helping clients uncover the life trauma that led them to this point, one of the techniques she uses with them is a life-transforming "I am enough" mantra. She has her clients write these words on mirrors and Post-it notes and place them at eye level throughout their living space.

Reminding yourself that you are enough may sound rather silly and trite. But when you think about how the human psyche is affected by the DNA we're born with and the "tough love" behaviors put upon us as children by well-meaning adults in our lives who are only repeating behaviors put upon them as children, and so on and so forth, it should come as no surprise when self-loathing plays out in a myriad of ways.

And we can't forget the bullies who lurk around every corner on the school grounds and on the internet – young kids and adults who use words to destroy other people. It makes perfect sense that we need a convincing reminder at just about every stage in life that we are enough.

Think about the people who grew up on the wrong side of tracks in homes complete with neglect, violence, drug addiction, and alcohol, yet they rise up out of the ashes to live exceptional lives. At some point on their life path, someone recognized them for the exceptional human being they were, encouraged them to believe in themselves, and they did. Did you get what I just said? Someone told them they were good enough and they believed it. *Believe it.*

When you acknowledge and recognize that you are enough, you will blossom and flourish in your newfound sense of acceptance:

1. Compete Only with Yourself. In 1994, [5] Tonya Harding's figure-skating career and life as she knew it came to a screeching halt when she indirectly conspired with her husband and bodyguard to take down her competition, teammate Nancy Kerrigan, at the U.S. Figure Skating Championships. Harding began skating as a toddler, won her first national title in 1991, and was the first American woman to perform a triple axel jump in competition. The girl had proven she was a force to be reckoned with on the ice. So what transpired at the championships that year with the whack heard

---

[5] https://olympics.com/en/athletes/tonya-harding

around the world, followed by Nancy Kerrigan's "WHY? WHY? WHY?" sobs shocked everyone. Tonya, for the second time, found herself lagging behind Nancy, and instead of upping her own game, she focused on beating Nancy – literally. At the end of a practice session, Nancy Kerrigan was struck above the knee with a police baton by Shawn Eckardt, a co-conspirator with Tonya's husband, Jeff Gillooly. Tonya later confessed to having knowledge of the plan, yet she did nothing to stop it.

As a dramatic example of competition gone completely awry, it's a great lesson in what can happen when we compare ourselves with the perceived competition and stop focusing on improving our own performance.

"I'm not in competition with anybody but myself. My goal is to beat my last performance."
-Celine Dion

Think about nature. No two flowers are alike and they don't waste precious time worrying about how to grow taller and be more beautiful than the other flowers in the garden. There's no peeking up through the soil to check out the "competition." They do the work required of them to display their greatness, which is soak up the nutrients from the earth, take in the moisture Mother Nature provides, absorb the warm rays of sun – and bloom.

Like Celine Dion, stay focused on beating your last performance and bloom where you are planted.

2. Expect Great Things. One day a little boy who was probably about eight years old came in to the dentist office where I worked. He was there

to sell candy bars, and his sales pitch went something like this: *"Hi, my name is Joey, and I have these chocolate candy bars I'm trying to sell. I don't know if they're any good and you probably don't want any. Some have nuts in them so I know I don't like them. They're two dollars which is probably too much money so I understand if you don't want to buy any – I wouldn't buy one either."*

I stood there in disbelief as he did his best to discourage me from buying a candy bar. He continued to ramble on, down selling the candy bars until I interrupted him and said, "I absolutely want to buy a candy bar from you." He looked at me in utter surprise and said, "Really? Okay. Thank you." And with little emotion, he took my two dollars, handed me the candy bar, and headed out the door. I didn't really want a candy bar, but the mom in me felt sorry for him and I wasn't about to let him leave without a sale. While it might have been the best sales ploy ever because, let's face it, I bought a candy bar, I rather doubt he won the award for selling the most candy bars, and he certainly didn't exemplify behavior that said, "Today, I am expecting to be the best candy salesman ever!"

"You must expect great things of yourself before you can do them."
-Michael Jordan

Little Joey needed a Michael Jordan in his life – someone to remind him to get up every day and employ his greatness. If you behave even a little bit like Joey, STOP IT! Think like Michael Jordan and expect greatness from yourself and the world you live in – every day and in every way.

3. Astound Yourself. My great niece just turned one, and she is actually speaking in complete sentences – astounding, right? Her mom recently posted a video of her singing her own praises with, "I did it!" every time she was successful in putting the block in the container she had busied herself with on that day.

"If we did all the things were capable of doing, we would literally astound ourselves."
-Thomas Edison

If anyone deserved the "I astound myself every day" award, it would be Thomas Edison. As a respected entrepreneur and inventor with over one thousand patents to his name, Edison pushed himself well beyond the limits of realizing his full potential, and yet it seems he still felt like he was capable of more. He never stopped inventing and didn't file his last patent until he was in his 80s. So what does that say about you and me?

When was the last time you astounded yourself with an "I did it" moment? Or have astonishing moments been relegated to the back corner of your mind and replaced with "Life is hard and then you die" mantras? This is the day to stop, turn to your right or to your left, and forge a new pathway that leads you on a route filled with astonishing self-moments.

As an anxiety-ridden society filled with insecurities that cause us to lose our way and forget that we are remarkable human beings capable of remarkable things, let me take this moment to remind you that YOU ARE ENOUGH.

At the end of the day, it's all about the D.A.N.C.E:

Do what your makes your heart sing. Do you look forward to getting up every morning and going to work? If not, find a new career – period.

Avoid negative energy. Surround yourself with positive people. Avoid toxic people and make no apologies.

Never give up. If at first you don't succeed try, try again. It's never too late for a do-over.

Choose happiness. Happy people are nicer people. Be happy.

Expect great things. Gratitude is the launching pad for attracting greatness. Be grateful.

About the Author

Melissa Liedkie is a marketing professional who has spent the last 30+ years developing winning marketing strategies for fortune 500 companies, and long the way she discovered a fascination for words and using them to tell stories.

She has authored a children's picture book, *Zane and Calli's Adventures in ThrowAwayLand.*

Melissa studied marketing and creative writing at Southern Methodist University (SMU.) She served as an Advisory Board Member for SMU's Advance Marketing Certificate Program (AMCP.)

Melissa lives in Grapevine, Texas with her husband.

"Throw kindness around like confetti."

———

RACHEL CORCORAN

www.ingramcontent.com/pod-product-compliance
Lightning Source LLC
LaVergne TN
LVHW010357300725
817250LV00040B/556